Got You!

Written and Illustrated by
Anna Grossnickle Hines

Children's Press®
A Division of Grolier Publishing
New York • London • Hong Kong • Sydney
Danbury, Connecticut

To my sister, Nelda
— A.G.H.

Reading Consultants
Linda Cornwell
Coordinator of School Quality and Professional Improvement
(Indiana State Teachers Association)

Katharine A. Kane
Education Consultant
(Retired, San Diego County Office of Education and San Diego State University)

Visit Children's Press® on the Internet at:
http://publishing.grolier.com

Library of Congress Cataloging-in-Publication Data
Hines, Anna Grossnickle.
  Got you! / written and illustrated by Anna Grossnickle Hines.
    p. cm. — (Rookie reader)
  Summary: Sam's older brother Mike keeps fooling him, but Sam thinks of a
way to turn the tables.
  ISBN 0-516-22176-0 (lib. bdg.)   0-516-27294-2 (pbk.)
  [1. Brothers — Fiction.] I. Title. II. Series.
PZ7.H572 Go 2001
[E] — dc21   00-029528

GROLIER
PUBLISHING

"Look out for the tiger!" said Mike.

4

Sam ran away.

"Got you!" said Mike.

"Look out for the bear!" said Mike.

Sam did not run, but he looked.

"Got you!" said Mike.

"Look out for alligators," said Mike.

"You can't fool me," said Sam.

"They are in the drain," said Mike.

"Got you!" said Mike.

Sam made a plan.
"I will get Mike," he said.

"Look out for the monster!" said Sam.

"You can't fool me," said Mike.

"Got you!" cried Sam.

"Good one!" said Mike.

Word List (37 words)

a	got	ran
alligators	he	run
are	I	said
away	in	Sam
bear	look	the
but	looked	they
can't	made	tiger
cried	me	will
did	Mike	you
drain	monster	
fool	not	
for	one	
get	out	
good	plan	

About the Author and Illustrator

Anna Grossnickle Hines's career with children began in the classroom, teaching preschool and third grade.

Then she turned her creative talents to writing and illustrating children's books. Many of the more than fifty books she has written and/or illustrated have received awards and honors. You can visit her website at www.aghines.com.